Tomorrow: Raising an Angel

Copyright © 2005 Claudia Vellozzi Averhoff & Francisco Averhoff

Memoir by Claudia Vellozzi Averhoff * Poetry by Monica Anne Averhoff

Published and released 2005 by Little Treasure Books

All rights reserved. No part of this publication – text or pictures – may be reproduced, stored in a retrieval system, or transmitted in any form or by any means – electronic, mechanical, photocopy, digital, broadcast, or any other except for brief quotation in printed or broadcast reviews, without written permission by the publisher. For permission please contact Little Treasure Books at www.littletreasurebooks.com.

Cover Book Design by Vanessa Vellozzi, San Francisco, CA * USA

Printed by ColorCentric Corporation, Rochester, NY * USA

Cover title: Tomorrow: Raising an Angel
ISBN: 0-9639838-8-1
Memoir / Poetry

TOMORROW: RAISING AN ANGEL

~ *Memoir by Claudia Vellozzi Averhoff*

~ *Poetry by Monica Anne Averhoff*

Remembering my sister,

    Although sisters can be annoying and a bother, my sister is the best in the world. Her twinkling eyes give a feeling of warmth and happiness. Under her bright smile is a sympathetic face. Curly, light brown hair surrounds her round face, giving her a happy and wonderful expression. Furthermore, her bubbly personality is only dampened when she is sad at rare but appropriate times. One may not believe this wonderful person could be any better, but there is even more to her than these many traits. In her loving nature, there is kindness, generosity, and comfort. I could not dream of a better sister than Monica.

Cristina Marie Averhoff

Tomorrow: Raising an Angel

ACKNOWLEDGEMENTS

Monica Anne Averhoff passed away at twelve years of age in a sudden and tragic accident. Following Monica's death, her Aunt Lorie found a notebook of poetry that unbeknownst to anyone, Monica began writing when she was ten-years-old.

"I remember Monica as a champion of justice, someone who was willing to stand up for what was right, and to be the one to come forward to speak in a delicate situation."

Susan Stengel
Former Principal Pattimura
Jakarta International School (JIS)

"Monica in her time with us taught us, nurtured us in her own way, and also gave us the courage and power to fly, reach out and maximize our lives. That is her legacy to us – that we should live as she did – fully and with purpose, spirit and love."

Hugh Collett
Middle School Teacher
Jakarta International School (JIS)

*"The end for me is in the wish to end **and they lived happily ever after**. But maybe this dissolving and this ache are a bitter lesson in the art of telling stories, to find relief not in her handsome prince and golden ever more, not in the direction of endings curlicued and seen from miles off, but just in the circle of listening, the shape things took, in a tiny sisterhood of hearts."*

Julie Orlemanski
Family Friend

"Monica was way beyond her years, much more mature than me. Monica was a lover, not a fighter. I know she changed my life. Her latest plan was to someday live in Swaziland Africa; she may be there now."

Lorie O'Connor
Monica's Aunt

"I miss you so much Monica! All of us (your friends over here) were just saying that if only we could see you one last time. I'll always remember you, and hope you remember us too."

Maita Mojica

"Memories of Monica:
>   Her love for her friends.
>   The constant wave of happiness when I would see her.
>   The fun times we had together.
>   The times we laughed and cried together.
>   Her care and respect for others.
>   The bad and good times we shared together.
>   The feeling in my heart that I get when I hear her name.

All these memories will stay in my heart and Monica will be there forever."

Austin Gary

"Our gratitude to Paula Yoon for her love and support, and for transcribing Monica's poetry."

"Our thanks to Bernadette Garzarelli, Publisher, for believing that Monica is an angel and that her poetry should be shared."

Claudia & Francisco

Tomorrow: Raising an Angel

Finally, with immeasurable gratitude to Francisco, dedicated husband and father, who continues to walk by my side in our shared loss and love. -Claudia

Tomorrow: Raising an Angel

DEDICATION

To Katie Jones, Monica's 5th grade teacher who inspired her to write.

To Austin to whom Monica dedicated her poetry.

And to all the parents who lost children as a result of one of the greatest natural disasters of our time, the tsunami of December 2004.

Tomorrow: Raising an Angel

Tomorrow
4/10/02

Tomorrow is a mystery,
Full of surprises.
We expect love to lead us to the right person,
To the right life.
But we drown in tears, if we haven't let ourselves learn to swim.

We might regret tomorrow,
If we let love carry us away on her back.
But if we can stand firm,
Love will find us.

Tomorrow we may land in a world of fantasies, dreaming.
Love might creep into our dream,
Not wanting to keep her distance.
She will transport us to the depth of our hearts,
Where you stand,
Waiting…

Tomorrow I might see you.
Not standing still, but beckoning.
I want to go and run into your outstretched arms,
Run and run and run away
From reality.

Tomorrow I can dance in your arms,
And we can share our love.

PREFACE

I used to tell Monica "I love you so much it hurts." And Monica, on more than one occasion, said "Mommy, I want to die before you because I don't think I could live without you."

These statements of love became a reality when Monica died suddenly at the age of twelve. In her short time with us she lived life to the fullest and knew what it was to love and be loved. We believe her poems reflect her sense of life and love, and share them with you in this memoir in the hope that you, too, will feel the love Monica gave all those whose lives she touched.

Claudia Vellozzi Averhoff

(All of the poems in this book were written by Monica. The story of Monica's life was written by her mother, Claudia Vellozzi Averhoff.)

Monica Anne Averhoff
September 2, 1990 – November 29, 2002

Tomorrow: Raising an Angel

Mystery Haiku
5/1/02

*Her wings made of glass
Rising up through the Heavens,
Peering at the world.*

*Faster and Faster
You can almost hear her heart,
Her soul is joyous.*

*Her smile, unhidden,
Tears of joy stream down her face,
Earth is crystal clean.*

*Her future is strong,
Going on for centuries,
It will never stop.*

FOREWORD

My daughter, Monica, must have been describing herself in the poem, "Mystery Haiku" on 5/1/02 when she was just eleven years old. I always knew Monica was special, but don't all parents think their first child is special and will live to fulfill their dreams? So many people, even my mother, would tell us how unusual Monica was, and that we were such good parents because she was well behaved and happy from the day she was born. It's not hard to be a good parent when your daughter is a living angel, and I believe that is what my husband and I did. We raised an angel, and I have no doubt that even though her life was cut short she remains an angel. A tattered spiral notebook of poetry we found after Monica was suddenly killed reassures us of this.

Monica's poetry is a legacy of the wisdom she so eloquently expressed through the eyes of a poet who lived a full life well beyond her years. Her notebook of insightful poetry that she began writing at ten years of age is a testimony to this.

Life
5/6/02

Drifting through the air,
Setting never,
Lighting up her spirit,
To the sky.

Swimming around,

Tomorrow: Raising an Angel

Giving herself to people,
Every day.
Taking herself away from people,
Every day.

Giving feelings to everyone.
She wants to give love, happiness, peace.
But hate, sadness and war always creep in.

Some of her gifts cause destruction,
To her.
Some of them
Make her fuller.

Without her we would never be,
Her spirit is what makes us exist.
She wants us to be grateful towards her.
She wants us to love her and live her
To the fullest.
She is life.

Chapter I

The beginning of Monica's life was far from typical. We were living and working for the World Health Organization in Geneva, Switzerland when I became pregnant with Monica. When I was thirty-seven weeks pregnant I was told that I had an infection called Toxoplasmosis. This illness during pregnancy is known to cause congenital abnormalities such as mental retardation, a small cranium, blindness, and other horrific afflictions in the fetus. I was immediately given potent medications that the child I was carrying would also have to begin taking at birth. The medicine would be continued into adolescence and if nothing manifested, this treatment would be discontinued. While being treated with this medication, weekly medical exams and blood tests would have to be performed. My husband and I were terrified and stressed, unable to sleep a wink for two weeks waiting for our daughter to be delivered or induced. The pediatric team would be ready to grab our newborn and perform all the necessary tests.

Distressed by the thought of being induced, we took a long train ride, hiked in the Alps, and returned to Geneva by train. The next morning I was rushed to the hospital and, with joy, quickly and naturally gave birth to Monica on September

2, 1990. Only the midwife and my husband were in the room. She immediately let out great cries, stretched, and started feeding. In our minds there couldn't possibly be anything wrong with this beautiful 5 lb., 11 ounce baby girl. However, our moment of relief was short-lived when the doctors showed up and whisked Monica away to be tested for infection and given medical treatment. We still could not believe this was happening since Monica seemed so normal and healthy. As there was actually no way of knowing for sure if the tests were accurate, treatments began immediately. After two days of a sad and stressful experience, the flood of tears came to a screeching halt. A physician we had met only once came into my room and told us to stop crying, that they had tracked down a blood sample taken during the first weeks of my pregnancy, and after comparing it to a recent blood sample determined that the test was a false positive! Suddenly awakened from our nightmare, I actually went to sleep for the first time in two weeks, so deeply that not even the wails of my newborn could arouse me. Our daughter was alive and healthy, and we were grateful.

Untitled
3/6/02

Sapphires
Beautiful blue
Glowing, shimmering, sparkling
My birthstone
Gorgeous

YOU
4/29/02

I love you in the morning,
I love you in the night.
I love you in the evening,
I love you during light.

I think about you always,
Even if you're not there.
Every single second,
Thoughts of you drift through my mind.
They are there and don't want to hide.

Sometimes I seem to wonder,
"Why are you on my mind?"
But I know the answer,
It's crystal clear,
You take up my heart,
And will always be there.

I have never felt this way before,
And never will again,
For you answer all my questions,
About love.

Chapter II

Monica had nineteen months of undivided attention by the time her sister, Cristina, arrived. She immediately took on the role of mother and big sister as she continually watched over Cristina. She loved that I breast fed Cristina because I would sit in the bedroom they shared and often read to Monica while Cristina satisfied her appetite. It was then that, to my amazement, Monica started reading to her sister. When we went to the pediatrician for Cristina's immunizations, Monica was not even two years old but proceeded to recite every nursery rhyme from one of her favorite books. It wasn't too long before she had an audience, and I realized that perhaps she wasn't really reading to Cristina but had memorized the book pretending to read from it. I'll never know for sure. This was just the beginning of her passion to read. By the time she reached third grade, Monica could read almost anything, challenging me with the problem of keeping her away from literature that was not age appropriate.

Untitled
3/1/02

You can go anywhere with books.
To Middle Earth,
To Oz,
To Oxford,
To Narnia,
You can go Beyond the Green Door
That was not left ajar.
You can travel on a magic carpet, too.

Monica and Cristina became two peas in a pod. Cristina took on many of the same interests that Monica had, and they played endlessly. Cristina also started reading voraciously, and so their library grew. Watching them grow was delightful; I simply needed to be around to keep up with their rapid development. Monica set the pace and led the way.

Wolf
4/9/02

Now a pup is born
Nestled in her mother's fur
Searching for her life

Playing with her mum
Following her mum's footsteps
Learning ways of life

Tomorrow: Raising an Angel

Wandering away
Trying to hunt by herself
Catching only mice

Growing up with friends
Learning to be an adult
Adulthood nearing

Trees never ending
Miles stretching before her eyes
She prances about

Tearing at the skin
Wolf struggles to keep alive
Winter is nearing

Dashing through the wood
Guiding her pups through a hunt
Curious eyes watch

Living in a den
New pups struggling for dear life
Feeling for their mum

Creeping upon prey
Ready to charge any time
The mother wolf won
Playing with her pups
Living life to the fullest
Keeping pace with them

Chapter III

Monica started school and not a day too soon for her, I might add. However, it did seem a little too soon for me. She loved school from the moment she entered the classroom. Challenge, structure, learning, achieving, and enthusiasm must have been part of Monica's makeup. She jumped in full force, and never slowed down. Her grades were excellent and she was always willing to help her fellow school mates. Our challenge was to make sure she remained stimulated, so ballet and piano lessons were added to her curriculum.

It was very early on that we noticed Monica's incredible passion for life and her desire to learn anything and everything. She used every waking moment to the fullest. And, she was happy. When she wasn't at school, Monica played school at home. Of course she was the teacher and Cristina and the American Girl Dolls were the students. Monica had decided that she would be a teacher when she grew up. By the time she was in middle school she had decided to one day become a university professor. As she grew older, Monica began challenging her teachers, but always with respect. She had an intensity and self-discipline about her that many of us never develop in a lifetime. As she grew, these traits grew with her. When Monica started middle school in Jakarta, Indonesia, the bus came at 6:20 in the morning. Realizing that in addition to learning to play the piano she wanted to stay after school to participate in the drama club and take ballet lessons, her solution to getting everything into one day was simply to start the day earlier. Most mornings she was the one waking us, playing the piano as early as 5 o'clock. We never asked her to get up so early; Monica was driven as if she knew there was no time to waste. She made time to email her friends, teachers, and family back home in Atlanta. In fact, Monica kept the family connected and made time for everything and everyone.

Time
4/28/02

We are pushing towards the end
Harder and harder.
Always fighting against her,
Wanting to relax
Going further and further
Into life.
Going on for centuries,
Without stopping.

Leaving behind marks,
In the weariness of people.

But, still,
We must win.

She is wrapping us inside her.
Encircling us.
Swirling towards the finish line.
Her strength,
Unwavering.
Time is like an opponent in a race.

Cristina always made sure that Monica had time to play with her. These were the times we heard giggling, watched them play dress-up, and listened to them talk about friends. Frequently we could hear Cristina scream, as Monica taunted her knowing just which buttons to push. Since Cristina was making more noise, our instinct was to be angry with her, but little by little we came to know who the instigator was. This happened mostly when Monica had a friend over to visit; after all she was so much older than her sister – 19 months and a whole grade older! Regardless, their love for one another was evident. They had a beautiful relationship and friendship with the joys and difficulties of being sisters. Since Monica was older she forged ahead of Cristina, making the way easier for her "little" sister. She let her know what to expect at school, what not to worry about and even kept her organized and on time. But most of all, she was Cristina's best friend and confidant.

Monica was also the leader. When it came to entertaining family and guests, she led the performances. The last Christmas we spent together was with another family who had two daughters. Monica designed and directed a program to entertain us, and together we enjoyed a wonderful performance of Christmas songs, piano, and costumes.

Chapter IV

At a very young age, Monica showed kindness to everyone however it was to my mother that she showed the most love and affection. Monica's grandparents came to Switzerland two weeks after Monica was born. My mother was the perfect granny, and held my daughter with such affection that they immediately bonded. Even the geographical distance between them couldn't stop this bond that grew stronger over the years. I used to bring the girls to visit grandma every six months. As my mom's health declined, Monica would crawl up into her bed, lay with her and hug her. Sometimes she read to her, but for the most part they would just laugh and talk. Monica was just 8 years old when her grandma died.

Grandma
4/30/02

That night so long ago,
Yet only yesterday.
Seeing her for the last time,
Lying there,
Helpless.

Her heart
Beating slowly,

Tomorrow: Raising an Angel

Too slowly.
As the minutes ticked by.

Then disappearing,
So suddenly,
As if she were a wisp of smoke,
Dying away.

She has left thousands of footprints in my heart.
They will never be washed out from rain,
No matter how hard it storms.

Chapter V

Monica spent a lot of time taking ballet lessons and made many friends along the way. She learned to dance with intensity and precision, all the while laughing with the other girls. This venue allowed her to express her confidence and self-discipline, which led to her becoming a role model. Our greatest challenge was getting her thick, curly hair into a bun. At ten years of age, she became part of the junior company in Atlanta, Georgia. Participating in the "Nutcracker" was the highpoint with this group of dancers. It was shortly after this performance when our family moved to Indonesia. My husband took a position working with the World Health Organization to help improve immunizations for children in Indonesia. Once in Jakarta, Monica continued to dance and started ballet lessons in a new and different setting. The dance studio was in a small, older house with no air conditioning. This was a challenge, as the climate in Jakarta is hot and humid. She was the only western girl in the class, which was taught in Indonesian. According to Monica the teacher was good, so none of this mattered . . . just one example of her true grit, commitment, and the drive to excel that she had for dance.

The first ballet recital was held in the Jakarta Civic Center. Three of Monica's friends and another family were there, applauding along with us. Having this support was important for Monica since she had a special part with her teacher who was a famous male dancer in his youth. It wasn't only Monica's performance that set her apart; she had the biggest smile and was the only non-Asian dancer on stage! Much later we learned that the performance had been video-taped when a friend of ours saw Monica bigger than life, dancing with her teacher on a large video screen at the entrance to one of the busiest shopping malls in Jakarta.

The Dancer
3/5/02

Arabesque, plea,
Batma fondue, passé
Frappe, fondue, fuette
These are some of the dancer's moves.
Step, Step, jete
Step, Step, jete
Grande jete,
Grande jete attitude,
A dancer practices her combination.

Arabesque turn,
Pirouette andeor.
Pirouette andedone,
Now back again.
Arabesque turn,

Pirouette andeor.
Pirouette andedone,
She practices her turns.

Monica was a good and loyal friend. Because her birthday was in September, she was older than the children in her grade. This, along with her self-confidence and sense of security, made her ability to maintain good friendships natural. Of course, there were the usual problems friendships encounter, but Monica seemed removed from these situations and was always involved in achieving the peace. She reached out to everyone. In Atlanta, two of her best friends were the youngest in the class and not part of the "popular crowd." Catie was quite shy but drawn to Monica who embraced her, and they became close friends during most of grade school.

In first grade, her friend Mary Kate wanted to spend her time exclusively with Monica, but Monica wanted to play with other friends too. At the time I was unaware of the problem this caused, but later came to learn that Monica creatively and diplomatically solved the problem on her own. She made a calendar for Mary Kate suggesting that they play together on Mondays, Wednesdays, and Fridays. On Tuesdays and Thursdays she would play with her other friends, of course welcoming Mary Kate to join in on those days. One evening I received a call from Mary Kate's mother who was upset that her daughter had come home crying because Monica made a calendar excluding her. I told her that I would speak with Monica before coming to any conclusions, knowing quite well that there would be more to the story. When Monica came home I asked her about the calendar. She looked up at me with her big trademark smile, explaining her version and showing me the calendar. It was then I realized that my young daughter could handle conflict with more thoughtfulness and tact than most adults. Monica and Mary Kate remained friends throughout her life and danced together for seven years.

When we were evacuated from Indonesia in October 2002 due to political conflicts, Monica reconnected with her girlfriends from the dance studio in Atlanta. They were all preparing for the "Nutcracker." I feared Monica may feel bad about not being able to participate, but of course I was wrong. She was never envious, and told me that we needed to see two performances of the "Nutcracker" so she could see both of her good friends perform. Monica wanted to see how much they had improved, was truly happy for them, and pleased to be together once again.

Together, Once Again
6/14/02

Coming together once again,
Walking further into life,
Together, once again.
Laughing together,
Once again.
Talking together,
Once again.

Sharing secrets,
Once again.
Playing together,
Once again.

Watching movies together,
Once again.
Bikng, roller-blading, scootering together,
Once again.

Just being together,
Once again.

Chapter VI

Monica thrived in Indonesia; she loved the environment, the different people, and the excitement of a school that offered classmates from many different countries. We had only been in Indonesia less than a week when her fourth grade class went on a field trip to a volcano in central Java.

Because we were in a developing country with climate, culture, and a society so very different from our own, I was a bit nervous but decided to let her go after speaking with her teacher and the mother who chaperoned the trip. She returned home, exhilarated and thrilled with the new friends she had made. The challenge of a new culture on the other side of the world was full of promise and adventure.

Paths
6/28/02

You have come to a corner,
My friend.
On the path
Of (your) life.

Stepping onto a new road,
Experiencing new things,
Having new adventures.

*But you will never forget
The path you left behind.*

*And one day,
You will come back.
Your footsteps will be on the path,
Guiding you.*

*And then you will move on.
You'll have new friends,
New teachers,
New people to enjoy.
But we are always behind you,
Following our own paths.*

*And one day,
We will all meet again,
Sometimes, maybe a hundred or ten hundred years away,
We will all be on the same path.*

Monica continued her after-school activities, primarily piano and ballet. We arrived in Jakarta nearly two-thirds of the way through the school year. Monica wanted to join the school dance club. The club performed for teachers and families in early May, and although March was already upon us, this didn't stop Monica. She spoke with the teacher and before long was choreographing her solo dance for the performance. I couldn't believe it! Not only was she ready, she was the only one to perform a solo. Monica had guts!

Playing the piano was another integral part of Monica's life. She was just a third grader when she was in a talent show. She played "Pachabel's Canon" bringing tears to my eyes and other adults in the audience. I watched in amazement as this nine-year-old played with poise and grace. She earned first place in the talent show that day.

The last piano piece she was practicing to perform at an upcoming recital was "Memory" from the Broadway play, "Cats." I remember waking up to the sounds of her playing this piece during our last weeks in Jakarta; unfortunately Monica never lived to play in this recital which was held two weeks after her death.

Moon
4/28/02

> Dancing before our very eyes,
> In a ball of light.
> The moon is like the keys of the piano,
> Playing her way across the sky.

Most of her friends were girls, but we did meet a boy she spent a lot of time with at school and at the Jakarta American Embassy Club swimming pool. Austin was small and sort of shy, sometimes feeling like a "geek." However, he found it easy to perform on stage and was in two plays while we were living in Jakarta. After we left Indonesia, he sent Monica an email telling her that if she liked another boy and he found out, he might turn back into the "geek" he was before meeting her. I believe these two young people loved one another in an adult kind of way, emotionally mature and with respect. I also think that some of Monica's poetry was inspired by her relationship with Austin, and later learned that she had dedicated a book of poetry to him.

Love is Amazing
3/13/02

Love is amazing.
We spend our whole lives longing for it.
But when we finally have it,
We are scared of the fact that it can waste away in a second.

Love is part of our lives everyday.
It seems as though everywhere we turn, there is love.
But when we seek it,
It seems as though lost.

Love is like the ocean.
It is calm sometimes,
And sometimes it is crashing.
But the ocean is always there.

The heart had represented love in our past,
Present, and future,
Our miseries, our happiness, our thoughts.

Tomorrow: Raising an Angel

*Love represents all of our feelings.
Even though it is a feeling in it self.*

Monica gave her all to relationships and activities in every aspect of her short life. She absorbed all that she could and demonstrated this in academics, music, and dance. I have much to brag about when it comes to my girls, but I know Monica wouldn't want that. Everything she did, she did with humility. These memories of Monica are forever a part of her father, her sister, and me. Like many parents, we live for our children and I can honestly say that Monica rewarded us time and time again.

FOR YOU I LIVE MY LIFE
5/7/02

*For you I live my life.
For you I give everything.
Forever in me,
You will be.*

*In the day,
I see you.
In the night,
I dream you.
Forever in me,
You will be.*

*When I am dancing,
Or playing the piano,
I see you clearly.*

Forever in me,
You will be.

Catching on like lightening,
Shining like the sea.
Forever in me,
You will be.

Flowing like a river,
Waiting like a rock.
Seeing you,
Makes my heart stop.
Forever in me,
You will be.

Standing tall like the mountain,
Blazing hot like the sun.
Forever in me,
You will be.

For you I live my life,
For you I give everything.
Forever in me,
You will be.

Chapter VII

As Monica matured, the early signs of her ability to bring diverse children together and promote cooperation manifested differently. Strangely, she never really 'grew' older but her behavior was 'adult-like.' It was as if she matured in fast forward. In fact, Monica's godfather, her Uncle Ray, predicted that she would one day become an Ambassador. The tragedy of September 11, 2001 may have influenced her thinking, especially since we were living in Indonesia where the population is 90% Muslim. It was then that she began to notice social injustices in the form of poverty, and prejudice in people of different ethnic and religious backgrounds. The ethnic Chinese Indonesians were disliked by the native Indonesians, Christians were disliked by the Muslims, and Americans were disliked by most everyone, especially after 9/11. Monica and her sister were both young when they learned a great deal about our world.

American personnel in Indonesia were asked to evacuate following 9/11 and then again a year later after Bali was bombed. Our family was intimately affected. These were stressful times for Americans living overseas in a Muslim country that was accused of harboring terrorists. Schools were closed, and when they reopened security was *intense; in an effort to secure safety, buses began taking alternate routes to the schools. Needless to say, our daughters had no choice but to grow up quickly.*

The Fairies
3/5/02

Through the trees and bushes,
Tiny winged people stare.
Their skin so soft, their feet so tiny,
But can you see their icy glare?
Pat, pat, pat, pat,
Their little wings make but a sound.
They fly away,
For us, never to be found.

Oh, but they can see us,
Though we may not them.
For you see, as quiet as we might be,
We have touched their faithful, protected gem.

Their gem is full of happiness and pride,
But now they must hide.
For the evil ogres are now glorified
While these tiny winged creatures are horrified.

But fear not! Tiny, little creatures.
The elves will come and make the ugly feature creatures
Have everything to fear,
While you steer clear
And cheer for your new shrine.

While elves and dwarfs may live in peace,

> While doves and sparrows too.
> Why can't our little fairy friends
> Live with the ogre like this too?
> Why must we all be at war?
> Why must we all not end,
> In a kind and loving area,
> Where peace and love
> Take us to the very end.

Despite the hardships, we lived well and Monica was happy, making good friends and soaking up everything she could. During our first summer in Indonesia we spent a month studying the language in Yogyakarta, a city in central Java; it was Monica who was best at communicating. She struck up a relationship and seemed to have a special bond with Toki, one of our housekeepers. They were kind to one another. Monica realized how poor Toki and her family were compared to us, and without reluctance passed her toys and clothes to Toki's daughter. Toki cried when she hugged Monica goodbye the last time we left Indonesia.

Although Monica saw the negative side of life, she remained optimistic. After being evacuated we lived in a small apartment, each of us with two suitcases waiting to hear if we would be able to return to Indonesia. One day when I was moping and complaining about our situation, Monica walked up to me with a glass of water, not quite full. She held the glass in front of me and asked me to describe it. I knew what she was getting at; was it half full or half empty? In her eyes it was half full so I drank it, and when it was empty we laughed together. Monica's optimism would never cease. Later I discovered the "Rules of Life" she wrote on May 28, 2002.

Rules of Life
5/28/02

Love life, you only get to live it once.
Live life to the fullest.

Live life for others.

It is better to be happy and have fun for five minutes, than to always be sad and bored.

Don't test people for friendship; trust that they will be good friends.
Feel lucky, even if you have only one friend, it is better than none.

Trust yourself.

Do what you think is best.

Give everything you can.

Always be optimistic.

Chapter VIII

Our first experience living overseas as a family was all Monica needed. This exposure only made her want more. Following our evacuation to the United States, we assumed we may not return to Indonesia. Monica immediately started suggesting alternatives, India or perhaps Africa. She always wanted more. While she enjoyed sharing experiences with her old friends, she made it a point to remain in touch with her friends in Jakarta. She loved and enjoyed all her friends and teachers in both countries, but was ready to move on. As a family we had grown so much closer; we were a tightly knit foursome, and I think all of us knew Monica led the way. She made me realize that we could go anywhere as a family and thrive. She set the tone; it was her enthusiasm that kept us going and encouraged us to consider another move overseas. It would be worth another move if just to watch our girls absorb more experiences.

Africa Poem
11/27/02

You carry on your head
Fruits of the jungle,
Trailing behind you
A monkey struggles.

On the sandy road you trek

Sore back, crick in neck,
Wishing you were home again.
You search for memories,
You find ten.

Stealing through the high mountain peaks,
Through the sandy Sahara desert.
A thousand birds show off their beaks
In the shining sun.

Shading your eyes from the sun's blazing rays
You must be lucky,
Living here all your days.

The passion for life Monica had was recognized by everyone. Living with a child who taught us daily how to give, how to remain optimistic, how not to judge others, how to be self-disciplined, was quite a gift. She brought us so much happiness; it was such a pleasure to travel, eat, shop, and do just about anything with Monica. She loved good food, not fast food, so taking her out to eat or cooking a fine meal was a pleasure. Unlike other children who were content eating grilled cheese sandwiches, Monica was a child who would rather have salmon for dinner and bring a salmon sandwich made from the leftovers to school for lunch. Sometimes she would bring lentils or beans for lunch, and joke about how the other girls groaned when they looked at her food. More than anything, Monica wanted to go to Italy and eat pasta and gelato.

We did go the summer before she died, and she was able to meet her great aunts, cousins, and extended family. Furthermore she learned to love cappuccino.

Untitled
3/6/02

Don't go back in time,
Don't live your life in the future.
Concentrate on the present,
So it is fit to give someone as a gift.

The Flowing Something
3/26/2001

Soaring high towards the sky
Something purple flows.
Could it be a busy bee,
Or something else?
Who knows?
I think it is my Father's hat, but really could it be?
It really looks like my roundhead,
But obviously, it's not me.

Chapter IX

Monica had a natural love for animals and nature. We had two dogs, and although she initially feared large dogs she was ultimately the one who would lay with her pets and take care of them as if they were her children. We got our first dog, a Dalmatian we named Cosmo, when Monica was seven years old. Both girls were very excited, but it was immediately evident that Monica would cower around the dominant male puppy. While teaching her how to be in charge, we would sometimes get angry with her but even angrier at the dog. In the long run, Monica learned how to control the dog and made up for all the discipline he received from us by caring for him intensely.

Cosmo
3/26/02

He stares at me with glaring eyes,
His glaze is harsh and icy cold,
But right inside he is sweet as a pie,
And he isn't nearly so bold.

His spots are like stars
Dabbing the sky.
But his tail is as white as a car
covered in snow and ice.
His coat is as soft as a blanket,
But his paws are as rough as sandpaper.
When there is a banquet,

Tomorrow: Raising an Angel

*He sneaks up and nabs food,
all except for the capers.*

*No matter if he is naughty,
no matter if he is nice,
I'll always love my baby Cosmo
who is made of sugar and spice!*

Chapter X

Watching and experiencing Monica mature was a special treat. As she entered adolescence she seemed to want to bond with me more than ever. She had reached the age of mom's best friend and teenager, while still a child. I began to confide in her and used to ask her opinion on clothes, work and many other things, to which she kindly and gently helped me and showed her support. She would tell me how beautiful I looked when I was dressing to go out, even when I thought I looked terrible, or encourage me to spend time at work even if it meant time away from her and her sister. I recall a time when I was deciding whether to continue a part-time business contract, and while Cristina was suggesting that I quit so I could be home more Monica was telling her that it was good for me to work and that they should encourage me to extend the contract.

Untitled
1/12/2002

Today I'm feeling sad,
I don't know what to do.
Mom won't let me go to Maita's
Or have her over here, too.
I don't know what I did.
But what it was, was bad.
So help me God, to understand.

Monica did go through the combative, "know-it-all" phase, which was most evident when her father would try to help her with homework. They locked horns, and at times it was quite a battle. While I thought this behavior would last for years, Monica surprised me once again and within two months this behavior stopped. Interestingly during this time she migrated toward me for reassurance and support; I always thought it would be the opposite. I noticed her confidence and trust in me, and her unconditional love. She respected my opinion and took it to heart.

Once when Monica was playing with some girlfriends at our house in Jakarta, the girls were dressing up and putting on make-up. Two of the girls happened to wear make-up regularly and clothes that I thought were a bit too mature for 12 and 13 year old girls. Monica had never even asked to wear make-up, and I made sure my daughters dressed appropriately. They willingly and happily agreed. During these dress up times, the girls were choosing clothes for Monica and making up her face. After her friends finished, she innocently came downstairs to show me how she looked. Through my eyes, she looked terrible; it was a look I certainly didn't want my daughter to have! I told Monica to go up and change immediately. The friend most responsible for this "costume" appeared. I didn't hold back, and was very stern with her. Monica didn't flinch. After the girls left I spoke with her; she wasn't angry or embarrassed. She actually felt I was right and was happy that I had intervened. I couldn't believe it, as I was expecting a battle or at the least, some anger. There was none. Monica trusted me and I was pleased, as any mother would be.

Feelings
3/6/02

Forever in my heart is love. It comes and goes but is always there when least expected.

Ever going.

Ever coming is happiness. Never there, yet always there. When there is need, we seek it.

Let your heart be open enough to let in the good.

Inside your heart is where you should be to find the answer.

No more should we seek from others to find what should be in your heart.

Giving you strength for your right to believe is your heart.

Sad, happy, excited, nervous, anxious, curious, loving, caring, kindness, are just some of the feelings we have everyday.

Chapter XI

As Monica approached adulthood there was a new sense of self-confidence and a fresh glow about her. She was happy to take that leap and was extraordinarily mature for her age. This became apparent as we read through her book of poems after her death. Perhaps she was inspired by her new, unique friendship with Austin. The emotions were tapped, and apparently Monica started letting these feelings flow.

Never Ending Kiss
6/4/02

Passing each other,
One foot,
Then the other.
Looking back,
"Did she see someone?"
Returning her stare,
Noticing someone's there.

An angel down from Heaven,
Shining through to Earth.
Landing down near her,
Someone who's worth.
Coming closer,
Shining brightly.
All of a sudden,
Holding her tightly.

Looking in each other's eyes,
Leaning closer, ever closer.
As she cries,
A tear of joy.

Heart beat racing,
Suddenly fading.
As they are embracing,
And kissed a never ending kiss.
As time stood still,
All around them,
They stood there with will,
Kissing their living gem.

Still embracing,
In their Heaven,
Living hell,
Though eleven.

"Summer's coming,"
So he thought.
"She will leave me,
but forget me not."

"I will miss him,
Dreadfully so.
But this memory,
Will not dim."

They kissed again,
With one last hug.
They will win,
In coming love.

Chapter XII

Monica's emotional development was coupled with her faith in God. A conscience to do good works began to manifest in her thoughts and actions. I think she placed God above everything and wanted to please Him. She also knew that God was watching over her. In one of her personal diaries she had drawn a heart, and inside the heart she wrote words representing the different issues in her life. Above the heart she wrote the word, "God." Her faith and gifts led her to approach life with love, passion and a desire to succeed. She wanted to volunteer-teach at an orphanage in Jakarta, travel more, and experience different cultures. She wanted to baby-sit and donate one dollar from every five she earned to a charity. She thought about war and prejudices. Yes, for her age Monica was different. She was also becoming aware of her limitations. A few months before she was killed, she asked me to tell her what her strengths were, excluding academics, so she could begin to focus on fewer activities. At just eleven years of age, she realized her desire to pursue her dreams and that it would be impossible to "do it all." I had a hard time answering her; she had so many strengths. It was then that I realized we can have expectations of our children beyond what we think is possible *and sometimes a child, like Monica, will rise to the challenge.*

The Bottle
4/7/02

Hidden, buried away in the depth of my heart,
is the bottle of thoughts,
holding my past, present, and future.

I have my grandma,
my angel.
Watching, looking with loving eyes,
upon me.
Peeping out of the bottle,
holding my past,
A stanza of clouds, moved on to a new sky,
Still the same sky, being far away.

I have the light of dancing,
my life.
Floating across the stage in a series of movement.
Swirling right out of the bottle,
Swimming with feelings,
Holding my present,
a car, on the way to my future,
a future, holding images in my mind.
Yet they are all swirling in a tornado,
ready to move on, if I do not grasp strongly enough.

I have dreams,
my secret universe.
Living there every moment of my day.

Tomorrow: Raising an Angel

Gushing out of the bottle with the speed of light,
Repeatedly whispering idea upon idea in my ear,
For only my soul to listen.

Holding my future,
The stars shooting their light at anyone who
Cares to wait patiently as they make their presence visible.
A colt, struggling with its first step,
then able to soar with the wind,
as it canters,
on and on.

Chapter XIII

Everyone seemed to notice something special about Monica. The parents of her friends welcomed Monica, and her aunts and uncles were always charmed by her. Teachers loved her because they recognized her thirst to learn and do well, whether it was piano, dance, academics or tennis. Monica touched many lives, the lives of her peers and adults alike. She especially touched those of us who were closest to her.

I Wish
3/24/2001

> I wish I was a sailing ship that floated on the sea.
> I wish I was a bright blue bird that hovered over me.
> I wish I was a quiet flower with radiant red petals.
> I wish I was some tea that is poured into kettles.
> But most of all,
> I wish that I will always be what I am now - free.

Monica connected with nature and animals. She enjoyed the school trips to the rainforests and rice paddies. Her experiences must have motivated her to dream and write about the world around her and her feelings of freedom in her world. Not surprising, her heaven was filled with animals. What was surprising was that she was able to express her thoughts with so much description and *emotion, as if she was actually having the experience, and maybe she was.*

The Flight of the Sparrow
3/26/02

In the vast field,
I spot a sparrow.
It is floating overhead,
with its wings slowly moving up and down like a leaf
swaying in the breeze.

It is unusually quiet almost as if all the life has gone,
but if you lay down and stretch out on the carpeted desert,
you can hear the frogs croaking and the insects buzzing.
The mice pattering and the snakes slithering.

I have drifted away from reality,
I can see myself standing in a glittering palace filled with
animals
each making their own and unique sound.
Every direction I turned,
there is a habitat for different animals.
Desert, ocean, meadow, swamp, river, creek, mountain,
rain-forest, forest, ice, trees.

I am awakened by the sound of a sparrow.
It seems as though calling to someone,
but it is only known to the spirits of the meadow.

I was surprised to see a cloud of sparrows
soaring through the sky.
Their wings flapping wildly at their sides.

*I stared up in bewilderment at the angels of the
Meadow, all dancing through the sky.*

*I wanted to call out to one of them,
ask them to take me with them on
their extraordinary adventure.
Over many meadows, oceans, deserts.
How at that moment I wish I could fly!*

*Then, one came swooping low,
too low,
It seemed to be motioning to me to come
and ride on its back.*

*I stood motionless,
Not knowing what to do.
It didn't seem to want to waste any time.
It glided through the air closer, closer....*

*And before I knew it,
I was gliding up above the clouds,
on the back of a sparrow.
All around me was blue,
a cool breeze rippled through my hair.
I was free!
I had a new freedom.*

*When I had gotten over my sensation,
we were in a glittering palace filled with animals,
each making their own and unique sound.*

Chapter XIV

Soon after we evacuated from Indonesia and returned to the United States, Monica had a sudden burst of development, becoming an adult in what seemed like overnight. We were back in Atlanta, Georgia in temporary housing for just over a month when Thanksgiving arrived. We decided to spend the holiday weekend at the beach in Florida, just the four of us and our two dogs. Still exhausted from our hectic travels, we simply needed a break.

Thanksgiving Day was one of the best I can ever remember. We were in a rental beach house, each participating in creating our Thanksgiving meal. Cristina and I made all the fixings while my husband took care of the turkey. Monica wasn't much of a cook, so she decided what would be on the menu making sure her favorites, stuffing and pumpkin pie were on it. Having finished directing the cooking cast, she stretched out on the sofa and read.

It was the day after Thanksgiving, and we decided to let the girls take a leisurely horseback ride on the sandy beach for an hour. The girls had been riding before, and were looking forward to viewing the ocean from atop the horses. It was on this ride that

Monica had a fatal accident, falling from her horse.

Mystery Haiku
4/26/02

Again and again
Sweeping low from the night sky
Then back up again.

Floating on the sky
Leaving behind her worries
Enjoying the day.

She is gone into
The Horizon, not to be
Seen for a long time.

I sometimes wonder if Monica knew her life would be short. She worked so hard every day to give everything she could and touched many hearts in the process. Some of the poetry she wrote seems to indicate there was an uncanny knowledge of her limited time on earth. Perhaps because of her spirituality and having been raised a Catholic, she wrote what seems to be about heaven. Her imagination frequently took her to a better place and gave her freedom.

Chapter XV

Monica's description of heaven and freedom in the months prior to her death is a bit unusual. The mere fact that a child her age wrote so much in such a short amount of time, with the insights and emotions of an adult, unaware that she would die suddenly from a tragic accident with no warning at all, is of itself unusual. Furthermore, some of her words were almost prophetic. Monica was capable of describing the reality of death for those left behind.

Every Time
5/2/02

Every time I look at you,
I see an angel in your eyes.
He flutters without stopping,
Wanting me to notice you.

Every time I talk to you,
I hear an angel in your voice.
He flaps his wings so hard,
That the noise comes out in your laughter.

Every time I'm near you,
I feel an angel in your midst.
He is hovering overhead,
Watching us ever so closely,
Noticing something.

Every time I look at you,
Every time I talk to you,
Every time I'm near you,
I notice something too.

On several occasions just months before she was killed, Monica would look at me and say "Mommy, I have to die before you because I don't think I could live without you." I reacted by smiling and telling her she was crazy and it was me who could not live without her. Of course I didn't take her seriously. Parents always die before their children.

In one of her poems she describes the sudden death of a sister, caused by head trauma (which is what took her life) as the two siblings were running together in a race. This is the only poem she wrote that ends with "The End". The poem is tragic, sad and horribly familiar, as if she knew what was going to happen in her own life and her sister's life, but as always, Monica's optimism can be seen, as she assures us that they will be together again.

Tomorrow: Raising an Angel

Untitled
8/18/02

*They loathed each other
So much, you could see
Venom coming out of their eyes,
And even their knees.*

*They'd stare at each other
With hatred so strong,
You could have sworn
The birds had stopped singing their song.*

*So one day,
They both joined a race.
"I'm going to win" one said.
The other, "I'll finish this case."*

*Three, two, one,
They were off,
Running ahead,
When one fell down,
Cracking her head.*

*The others looked back,
And kept on running,
But her enemy said,
"Wait, I'm coming!"*

*He called an ambulance,
Told them to come.
"You'll have to hurry,
This won't be much fun."*

They took her away,
With him at her side,
He stayed there one day,
Forgetting his pride.

A knock at the door,
He opened his eyes.
The doctor was there,
Then he started to cry.

"Doctor," he said
Between all his sobs.
"She can't be dead!"
The doctor gave a nod.

"I'm sorry, dear boy,
But the truth is the truth,
Your sister is dead,
That's the end of her youth."

"But I didn't say,
'I love you' one last time,
or hold her in my lap
and give her a dime."

"I'm sorry, I said,
But the truth is the truth.
You'll have to live without
Your dear Ruth."

He wept on Ruth's arm,
And kissed her forehead.
"I'll love you forever,
I wish you weren't dead."

Tomorrow: Raising an Angel

*Then all of a sudden,
A bright light appeared
"Brother Tom, I'll be waiting in Heaven
for you."
Then the light just disappeared.*

The End

Chapter XVI

A year and a half after we lost Monica I came across an excerpt from "The Death of the Young," written by Tolstoy in which he captures the essence of a short accomplished life, a life that Monica lived.

"The Death of the Young"

People ask: "Why do children or young people die, when they have lived so little?" How do you know that they have lived so little? This crude measure of yours is time, but life is not measured in time. This is just the same as to say, "Why is this saying, this poem, this picture, this piece of music so short, why was it broken off and not drawn out to the size of the longest speech or piece of music, the largest picture?" As the measure of length is inapplicable to the meaning (or greatness) of productions of wisdom or poetry, so – even more evidently – it is inapplicable to life. How do you know what inner growth this soul accomplished in its short span, and what influence it had on others?

--from <u>Spiritual Life Cannot be Measured</u> by Tolstoy

Tomorrow: Raising an Angel

Francisco & Claudia Averhoff, Cristina (left) Monica (right) and the Family dogs – November 29, 2002